Table of

Contents

getting started

24

22

projects

27

30

welcome

Learning something new usually requires some instruction. You might take a class, work with a friend, or read up on the subject in a book or magazine. One way or another, you'll need to gain the necessary skills to get started.

If you're new to quiltmaking, you've already begun the learning process by picking up this publication. Packed with basic quilting how-tos and numerous tips, *1-2-3 Quilt* also helps you apply what you learn with a variety of easy and exciting projects, including quilts, wall hangings, a handy tote, and a trio of pillows. Let's get started—the fruits of your newfound skills are yours to enjoy and share!

Tools of the Trade

Having the right tools on hand will make quilting even more fun.

Rotary-Cutting Tools

Rotary cutters have round blades that enable you to cut straight-edge shapes more quickly and accurately than scissors can. They come with various blade sizes—a good size for a first blade is 45 mm. Experiment with handle styles to see which you prefer.

For making perfectly straight cuts, choose a thick, clear acrylic ruler. A good size to start with is a 6×24" rectangular ruler marked in ¼" increments.

Always use a rotary cutter with a cutting mat specifically designed for it. In addition to protecting your work surface, the mat helps keep the fabric from shifting while you cut. Start with a 17×23" mat marked with a 1" grid, hash marks at ⅛" increments, and 45° and 60° angles.

Fabrics

The best fabric for quiltmaking is 100% cotton because it minimizes seam distortion, presses crisply, and is easy to quilt. Our instructions specify quantities for 44/45"-wide fabrics unless otherwise noted. We allow for a little extra yardage to accommodate minor cutting errors and slight shrinkage.

There are conflicting opinions about the need to prewash fabric. The choice is yours, but if you have any doubts about colorfastness, test the fabric before adding it to your quilt.

Threads

For piecing and most quilting, match the thread fiber to the fabric. Since most quilters use 100% cotton fabric, 100% cotton thread is ideal. If you find your thread breaking, try a new spool; old thread can become brittle and lose elasticity.

Needles

The preferred needle type for woven cotton fabrics is called a "sharp." Sizes 75/11 and 80/12 are good choices for piecing, quilting, and binding most quilts. Use a smaller needle (70/10) if you're piecing tightly woven batiks and a larger needle (90/14) for flannels. Dull needles can cause skipping or uneven stitches, so it's a good idea to insert a fresh needle at the start of every project.

Sewing Machine

Any machine with a straight stitch and well-adjusted tension (not too tight or too loose) will work for piecing. A machine that also can zigzag- or blanket-stitch makes machine appliqué possible. If your machine has bad stitch quality, before making any other adjustment, lift the machine's presser foot and rethread the machine.

Use cotton thread for cotton quilts; the fibers will be equal in strength and should wear evenly.

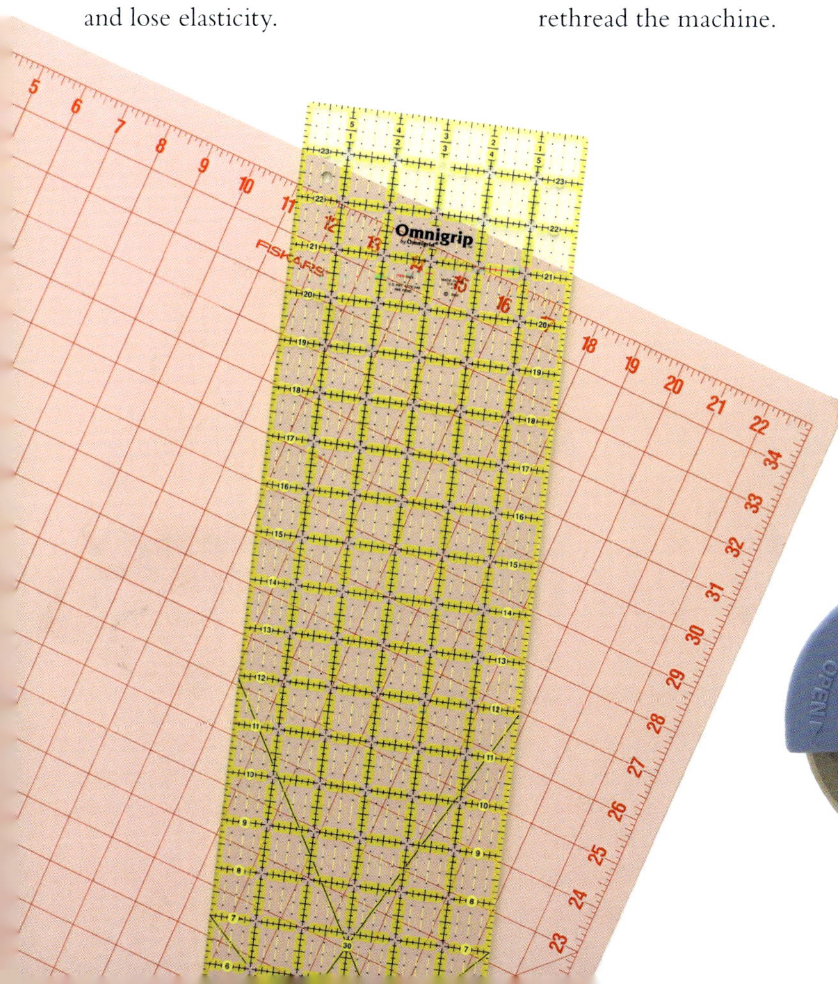

Rotary-cutter blades are extremely sharp. Develop a habit of closing or retracting the blade after each cut, or buy a cutter with a self-retracting blade.

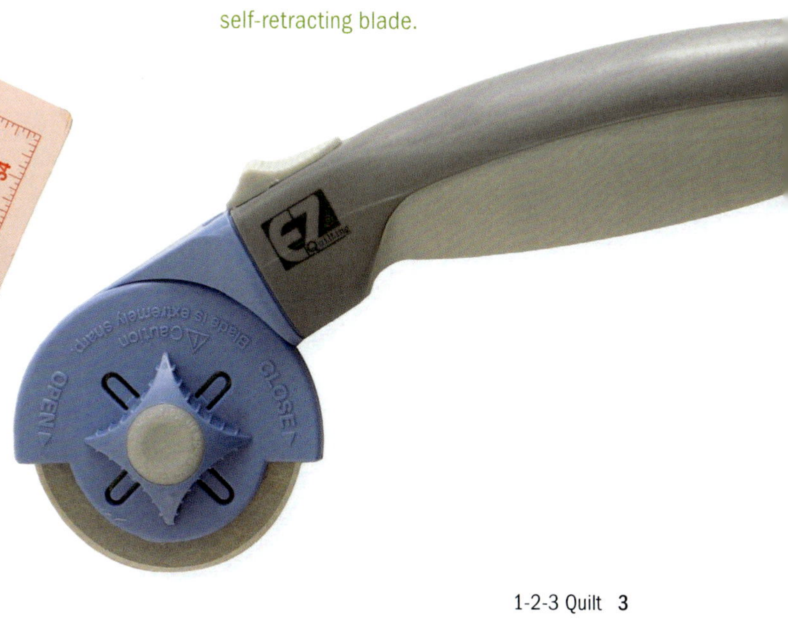

Choose Fabrics with Confidence

Take the fear out of selecting just the "right" fabrics for your quilt by learning to audition them first.

Whether you're selecting scraps from your stash or buying all the fabrics for a project at once, the array of colors and designs can be both exciting and intimidating. While there are no "wrong" fabric choices, some combinations are more pleasing to the eye than others. If you can't seem to make up your mind about which fabrics to use, read on!

Begin the Search

Separate the fabrics you're interested in and examine them away from other fabrics to avoid confusion or interference from other colors.

Find optimum light. Fluorescent light can sometimes cast a yellow glow, altering the appearance of a fabric's true colors. At home, work during daylight or consider investing in a lamp that simulates sunlight. If you're at a quilt shop, take the bolts to the area that has the most natural light. Stand with the light at your back and let it wash across the bolts.

In the store, stack bolts horizontally to view how fabrics work together and how they may appear when cut into smaller shapes. Stand back about 10 feet and look at the stacked bolts; a view from this distance will give you an idea of how a fabric combination will work.

For an even better preview of what individual pieces of a fabric will look like, view the print through a template window (Photo 1). Cut the desired shape out of sturdy paper or cardboard. Don't include seam allowances, but do leave a healthy margin of paper around each window to help differentiate what's showing through from the rest of the bolt.

In addition to color, it's often contrast (difference in values) that makes a quilt design successful. Without contrast, block pieces or whole blocks can blend together and the design will be lost. Try squinting at your selected fabrics—this makes contrast more evident. If the colors seem to blend together, substitute lighter or darker fabrics until you have a variety of values. If a certain print is too dominant and jumps out at you, you may have too much contrast.

Fine-Tune the Fabric Mix

Once you've selected a few fabrics, combining them successfully takes patience, experience, and a willingness to just play around with the fabrics.

One of the best ways to tell if your fabric combination will work is to step back from it. Fabrics that don't

Photo 1

Photo 2

Photo 3

COLOR-SELECTION TROUBLESHOOTING

IF YOU DON'T KNOW WHERE TO START:

- Read quilt books and magazines, studying the designs you like best.
- Use a favorite fabric as a starting point for choosing others.
- Join a quilt guild for inspiration and advice from fellow quilters.

IF YOU LIKE A QUILT PATTERN BUT DON'T LIKE ITS COLORS:

- Study color combinations in favorite articles of clothing.
- Look at home decorating magazines for color inspiration.

IF THE FABRICS YOU'VE CHOSEN HAVE NO COLOR CONTINUITY:

- Replace some of the stronger colors with their muted versions.
- Try adding a complementary color.
- Choose a dominant fabric to use in the blocks and borders, unifying the overall design.
- Add neutrals or less-intense colors to give the eye a place to rest.

appear to work when viewed up close may be perfect from a distance, where you can see a single fabric's contribution to the whole. Remember that each piece is just a fraction of the total finished product.

Test your block design and fabric selections by mocking up a block. Cut fabric pieces for one block to the finished size (leave off the seam allowances; these test pieces won't be used in the finished project). Sketch the block design on graph paper, and glue the fabric pieces on the paper to create a mock block (Photo 2, *page 5*).

Place the block several feet away to view the design and color combination. If desired, make additional blocks to test alternate fabric choices. To further test the color and layout, make color photocopies of the mock block (Photo 3, *page 5*). Use the copies to begin planning the quilt top. Keep an eye out for patterns that emerge based on how you turn the blocks. Check color placement in adjacent blocks and make sure you like what's happening.

Having a vertical surface to lay out fabric choices can help you visualize how they will look in a quilt. For a permanent design wall, cover a foam-core board with a neutral flannel to hold small pieces in place, as shown on *page 4*. You also could use the flannel back of a vinyl tablecloth, rolling it up between projects or hanging one in front of another to view different quilts that are in progress.

WHAT IS A FAT QUARTER?

A fat quarter is ¼ yard of fabric cut in a different shape than the traditional ¼-yard piece of 44/45"-wide fabric. While a traditional ¼-yard cut is narrow and long (9×44"), a fat quarter is nearly square (18×22"). Many quilters like the cutting options offered by a fat quarter. To get a fat quarter, a ½-yard fabric piece is cut in half crosswise, making two "fat" quarter yards. Found in most quilt shops, fat quarters (and fat eighths, which measure 9×22") are sold individually or packaged in bundles of a specific fabric line or color palette.

IS ANYTHING MISSING?

Variety in fabrics results in an eye-catching quilt. After you've selected the fabrics for a project, ask yourself these questions about the combination's contrast, color, and character to see if you've achieved variety and what might be missing.

- Do I have a variety of light-, medium-, and dark-value fabrics for the blocks, appliqués, and overall quilt top?
- Have I selected colors according to a certain color scheme or grouping of color families—such as primary (red, blue, yellow), secondary (orange, violet, green), complementary (opposites on the color wheel), or tertiary (combination of primary and secondary colors, such as red-orange or blue-green)?
- Did I include shades (where black is added for a darker color) and tints (where white is added for a lighter color) of the color families that are represented?
- Do the fabric intensities work well together?
- Did I include small-, medium-, and large-scale prints?
- Have I chosen a variety of print styles?
- Is the mood of the fabrics right for the quilt I want to make?

What Are Templates?

A template is a pattern made from extrasturdy material so you can trace around it many times without wearing away the edges.

To make templates, use easy-to-cut template plastic, available at quilt shops and crafts supply stores. Its transparency lets you trace the pattern directly onto its surface.

1. To make a template of a specific pattern, lay template plastic over the pattern and trace the solid outside edges, dashed seam lines, and grain-line arrow onto the plastic using a permanent marker and ruler. (An arrow on a pattern indicates the direction the fabric grain should run.) Mark the template with its quilt name, letter, and any marked matching points (Photo 1).

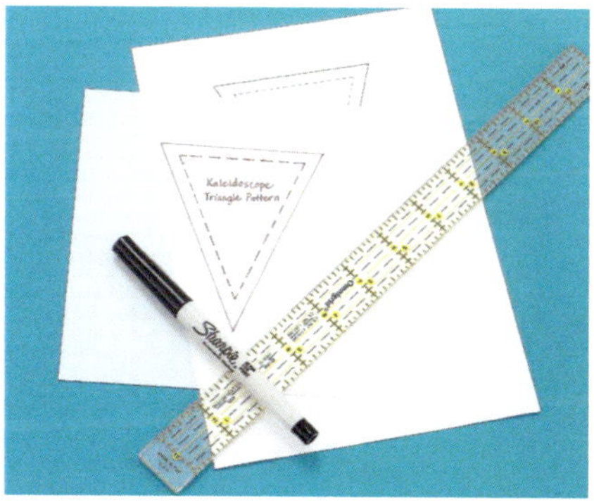

Photo 1

2. Cut out the template and check it against the original pattern for accuracy (Photo 2). If it isn't accurate, the error (even if it's small) will multiply as you assemble a quilt.

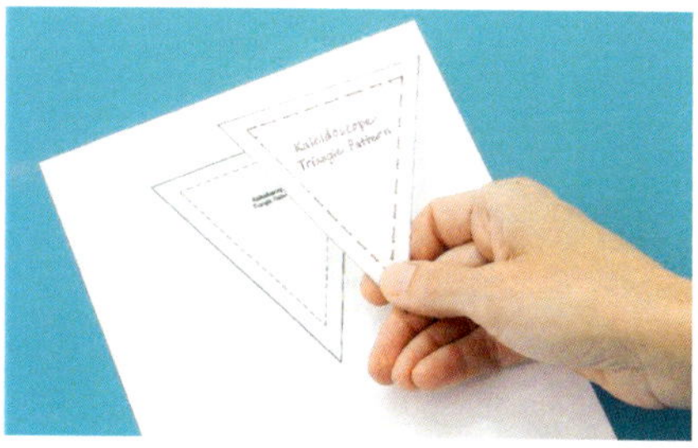

Photo 2

3. Using a pushpin, make a hole in the template at all marked matching points (Photo 3). The hole must be large enough to accommodate a pencil point.

Photo 3

4. To trace the template on fabric, use a pencil, a white dressmaker's pencil, chalk, or a special fabric marker that makes a thin, accurate line. Avoid using a ballpoint or ink pen, which may bleed. Test all marking tools on a fabric scrap before using them. Place your fabric right side down on 220-grit sandpaper to prevent the fabric from stretching as you trace. Place template facedown on the wrong side of the fabric with the template's grain line parallel to the fabric's lengthwise or crosswise grain. Trace around the template. Mark any matching points through the holes in the template (Photo 4). (When sewing pieces together, line up and pin through matching points to ensure accurate assembly.)

Photo 4

5. Repeat to trace the number of pieces needed, positioning the tracings without space between them. Use scissors or a rotary cutter and ruler to precisely cut fabric pieces on the drawn lines (Photo 5).

Photo 5

Rotary Cutting

Successful quilt construction requires precise cutting. With accurately cut pieces, even a beginning quiltmaker can assemble a quilt with ease. Gaining mastery of a rotary-cutting tool can make all the difference in your quiltmaking experience.

With a rotary cutter, you can make accurate cuts through multiple layers of fabric. One of the strongest appeals of rotary cutting is the precision and speed with which you can cut multiple strips, squares, triangles, and diamonds, thus enhancing your enjoyment of the quiltmaking process.

TIP

Bend at the hip rather than at the waist when rotary-cutting—it is easier and puts less stress on your back and arms. To help you with this, place your cutting mat on an appropriate height table or countertop.

As with many techniques, the more you practice the easier and more natural the process will become. Practice rotary cutting on fabric scraps until you develop confidence in your cutting accuracy.

Tool Basics

To rotary-cut fabrics, you'll need three basic pieces of equipment—a rotary cutter, acrylic ruler, and cutting mat. A rotary cutter should always be used with a cutting mat designed specifically for rotary cutting. The mat protects the cutting surface and keeps the fabric from shifting while it's being cut.

Cutting mats usually have one side printed with a grid and one side that's plain. To avoid confusion when lining up fabric with the lines printed on the ruler, some quilters prefer to use the plain side of the mat. Others prefer to use the mat's grid.

The round blade of a rotary cutter is razor sharp. Be sure to use a cutter with a safety guard and keep the guard over the blade whenever you're not cutting. Rotary cutters are commonly available in three sizes; a good all-purpose blade size is 45 mm.

For more information on the tools needed for rotary cutting, see Tools of the Trade, *page 2*.

Squaring Up the Fabric Edge

Before rotary-cutting fabric into strips, it is imperative that one edge of the fabric be straightened, or squared up. Since the accuracy of all subsequent cuts depends on this first cut, squaring up the fabric edge is a critical step.

There are several ways to square up fabric—here, we show the single-ruler technique. Instructions are given for right-handed cutting.

Squaring Up with the Single-Ruler Technique

This method requires just one ruler, but you must turn the mat or move to the opposite side of your cutting surface after squaring up the fabric before you can cut strips.

1. Lay the fabric right side down on your cutting mat with one selvage edge away from you.

2. Fold the fabric in half with the wrong side inside and the selvage edges together.

3. Fold the fabric in half again, aligning the folded edge with the selvage edges. Hand-crease all folds.

4. Position the folded fabric on the cutting mat with selvage edges away from you and the bulk of the fabric to your left.

5. With the ruler on top of the fabric, align a horizontal grid line with the lower folded fabric edge, leaving about 1" of fabric exposed along the right-hand edge of the ruler.

Do not try to align the uneven raw edges along the other side of the fabric. If the grid lines on the cutting mat interfere with your ability to focus on the ruler grid lines, turn your cutting mat over and work on the unmarked side.

6. Hold the ruler firmly in place with your left hand, spreading your fingers apart slightly and keeping them away from the right-hand edge of the ruler. Apply pressure to the ruler with your fingertips. (Some quilters keep their little finger just off the ruler edge, pressing it on the cutting mat to stabilize the ruler.) With the ruler firmly in place, hold the rotary cutter with the handle at an angle to the cutting mat and the blade abutted

ROTARY-CUTTER TROUBLESHOOTING

Is your cutter not cutting through all the layers? Check the following:

- Is the blade dull? If so, replace it and carefully dispose of the used one. Some blades may be successfully sharpened with a special tool.
- Is there a nick in the blade? You'll know if you discover evenly spaced uncut threads, the result of a blade section not touching the fabric during each rotation. Replace the blade. In the future, avoid cutting over pins and/or dropping the rotary cutter.
- Did you use enough pressure? If you don't have a dull blade but still find large areas where fabric layers weren't cut through cleanly, or where only the uppermost layers were cut, you may not be putting enough muscle behind the cutter. If the problem persists, try cutting fewer fabric layers at a time.
- Is your mat worn out? With extended use, grooves can be worn into your cutting mat, leaving the blade with not enough resistance to make clear cuts through the fabric.

against the ruler's right-hand edge. Roll the blade along the ruler's edge, starting your cut just off the folded edge and pushing the cutter away from you, toward the selvage edges.

7. The fabric strip to the right of the ruler's edge should be cut cleanly away, leaving you with a straight edge from which you can measure all subsequent cuts. Do not pick up the fabric once the edge has been squared; instead, turn the cutting mat to rotate the fabric.

8. Begin cutting strips, measuring from the cut edge.

Cutting Squares or Rectangles from Strips

Use a rotary cutter and strips of fabric to cut multiple squares and rectangles accurately and quickly.

1. To cut squares, cut fabric strips that are the desired finished measurement of the square, plus ½" for seam allowances. For example, for 3" finished squares, cut 3½"-wide fabric strips.

2. Square up one end of each strip (instructions begin on page 8).

3. Using a ruler, align a vertical grid line with the cut edge of a fabric strip. Align the top and bottom edges of the fabric strip with the horizontal lines on the ruler.

To cut squares, cut the fabric into lengths equal to the strip width. For example, for 3" finished squares, cut the 3½"-wide fabric strips into 3½"-long pieces.

4. To cut rectangles, cut fabric strips that are the desired finished length, plus ½" for seam allowances. For example, for 3×5" finished rectangles, cut 3½"-wide fabric strips into 5½" lengths.

CUTTING STRAIGHT STRIPS

When you're cutting several fabric strips in succession, it's possible for your ruler to get slightly askew, causing your strips to be crooked. How will you know? When you open a strip, there will be a slight swerve or bump at the center fold line.

To avoid cutting multiple crooked strips, stop every few strips when you're cutting and open them up. If you discover a bump in the middle, square up your fabric again before cutting any more strips.

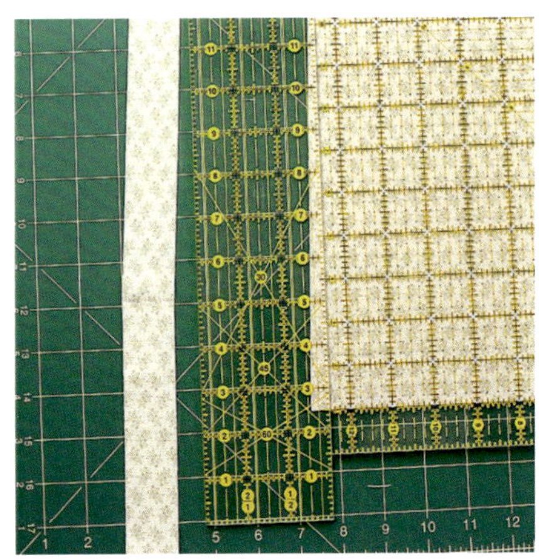

Cutting Triangles

Right triangles can be quickly and accurately cut with a rotary cutter. Learn these two common methods.

Many quilts are made up of a variety of half-square triangles (two triangles cut from one square) and quarter-square triangles (four triangles cut from one square). Cutting directions for quilts in this issue will tell you to rotary-cut triangles in one of two ways.

If you need to cut half-square triangles, the instructions will say something like this:

From bright coral print, cut:

- 2—8⅞" squares, cutting each in half diagonally for 4 large triangles total

First cut squares in the size specified in the directions. Then line up a ruler's edge with opposite corners of a square (Photo 1). Cut along the ruler's edge to cut the square in half diagonally; separate the triangles. Repeat with the remaining squares. Because the triangles' long edges are on the bias, avoid stretching them when piecing so you don't get distorted seams.

Photo 1

If you need to cut quarter-square triangles, the instructions will say something like this:

From green print, cut:

- 2—9¼" squares, cutting each diagonally twice in an X for 8 small triangles total

First cut squares in the size specified. Then line up a ruler's edge with opposite corners of a square (Photo 2). Cut along the ruler's edge to cut the square in half diagonally, but do not separate the two triangles created. Instead, line up the ruler's edge with the remaining corners and cut along the ruler's edge to make four triangles total; separate the triangles. Because the triangles' short edges are on the bias, avoid stretching them while piecing so you don't get distorted seams.

Photo 2

Cutting on the Bias

Cutting on the bias is a useful technique for piecing, binding, and appliqué. Learn how and when to apply it.

Bias runs diagonally between the lengthwise and crosswise grain line of a woven fabric. The "true" bias runs exactly at a 45° angle to the grain lines (Fabric Grain Diagram) and has the most stretch in a woven fabric.

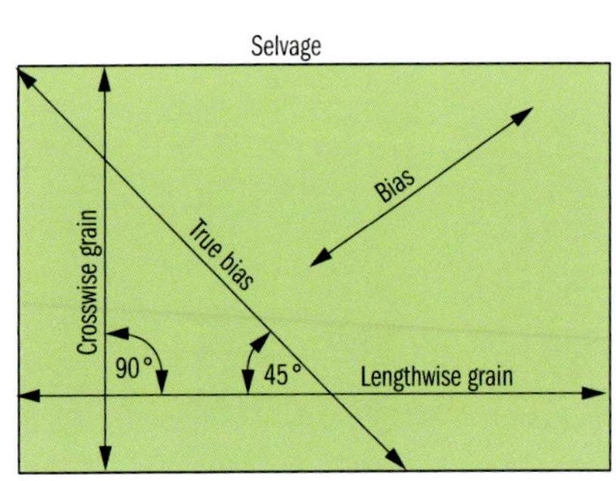

Fabric Grain Diagram

When should I cut on the bias?

Because of their built-in stretch, strips cut on the bias can be easily curved or shaped. Use them when binding curved edges or to make curved appliqué pieces such as vines or stems.

You also can cut directional fabrics such as plaids or stripes on the bias for purely visual reasons. A bias binding or border cut from a stripe creates a "barber pole" effect.

How do I cut bias strips?

Begin with a fabric square or rectangle. Using an acrylic ruler and rotary cutter, cut one edge at a 45° angle. Measure the desired width from the cut edge and then make a cut parallel to the edge. Repeat until you have the desired number of strips. Handle bias strips carefully to avoid distorting the fabric.

Piecing Fabrics

The keys to successful patchwork are practice and patience.

Precise ¼" seams allow you to join units, blocks, and rows with ease.

Stitching

Quilting depends upon accuracy at every step. Use exact ¼" seam allowances throughout a quilt's construction. It isn't necessary to backstitch at the beginning of any seam that will be intersected by another seam later in the quiltmaking process. Use a stitch length of 10 to 12 stitches per inch (2.0- to 2.5-mm setting) to prevent stitches from unraveling before they're stitched over again. Secure seams that won't be sewn across again (such as those in borders) with a few backstitches.

Pinning

When you want seam lines to line up perfectly, match up seams of pieced units and place an extrafine pin diagonally through the pieces, catching both seam allowances. Avoid sewing over pins.

Press seam allowances in each row in opposite directions so they abut when rows are joined.

Pressing

Pressing seams ensures accurate piecing. Set a seam first by pressing it as it was sewn, without opening up the fabric pieces. This helps sink the stitches into the fabric, leaving you with a less bulky seam allowance.

The direction you press is important and is usually specified in the instructions. Generally, you'll press the entire seam to one side rather than pressing it open. When two seams will be joined, press the seams in opposite directions; this helps the seams line up perfectly and reduces bulk.

Make sure you are pressing, not ironing. Pressing is lifting the iron off the surface of the fabric and putting it down in another location. Ironing means moving the iron while it's in contact with the fabric; this stretches and distorts seams.

Sewing Exact Seams

Successful machine piecing depends on sewing an exact $^1/_4$" seam. Learn how to set up your machine to sew accurately.

Seam guides make it easier to stitch an exact ¼" seam. The most common seam guide is a ¼" presser foot. Many machines offer this foot as an option. With this foot and the needle in the standard position, the edge of the foot serves as the seam guide.

Another seam guide option is placing layers of masking tape or moleskin on your machine bed ¼" away from the needle. When sewing, position the fabric along the tape (or moleskin) so it feeds under the presser foot and needle with an exact ¼" seam allowance (Photo 1).

Photo 1

Take the time to test your seam guide to make sure you will be sewing seams that are ¼" wide. Sew a sample seam with the raw fabric edges aligned with the right edge of the presser foot or up against the masking tape or moleskin.

Measure the resulting seam allowance using a ruler or graph paper with a ¼" grid (Photo 2). Make any adjustments necessary to achieve the ¼" seam allowance.

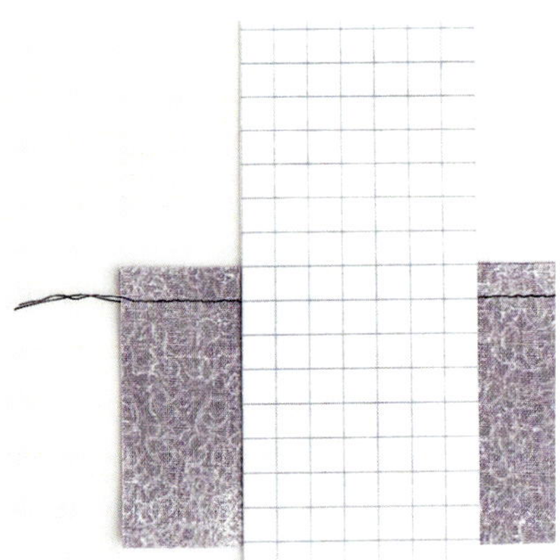

Photo 2

To practice sewing exact ¼" seams, cut three 1½"-wide strips of two contrasting fabrics. Sew together two of the strips using a ¼" seam allowance. Join the third strip to the first two, again using a ¼" seam allowance. Press seams away from the center strip.

Place the fabric right side up on a flat surface; measure the width of the center strip. If your seam allowances are accurate, the center strip should measure 1" wide (Photo 3). If your center strip doesn't measure 1" wide, you didn't sew ¼" seams. Move your seam guide as necessary and retest until you get a 1"-wide center strip.

Photo 3

Mitering Borders

Mitered corners (similar to corners on a picture frame) add a dash of drama to an otherwise plain border.

Cutting

When instructions specify mitered borders, cutting instructions include extra length needed to miter corners. However, if you'd like to substitute a mitered border for a standard straight border, cut strips the width (but not the length) specified.

For side border-strip length, measure through quilt center from top to bottom; then add twice the border width plus 6". For example, if your quilt measures 40" long and your border is 5" wide, you would cut your side border strips 56" long (40" + 10" + 6"). For top and bottom border-strip length, measure through quilt center from side to side; then add twice the border width plus 6".

Preparing

If you're adding multiple borders, first join border strips for each side into a single border unit.

Fold each border strip in half crosswise; press lightly to mark centers. Fold quilt center in half in each direction and press lightly to mark center of each edge.

Pin a border strip to quilt center edge, matching the center marks and allowing excess border strip to extend beyond the corner edges. Sew together, beginning and ending the seam ¼" from the quilt center's corners (Diagram 1).

Repeat to sew border strips to remaining edges. Press all seams toward border.

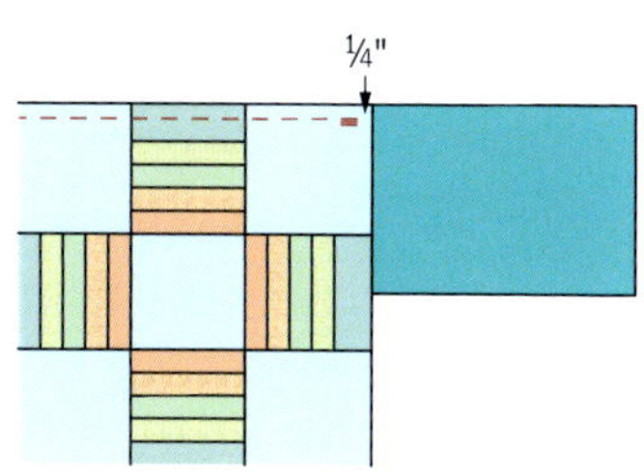

Diagram 1

Mitering

To miter each corner, lap one border strip over the other (Diagram 2). Align the edge of a right triangle with the raw edge of the top strip so the triangle's long edge intersects the border seam in the corner. Draw along the triangle edge from the seam out to the raw edge. Place the bottom border unit on top and repeat the marking process.

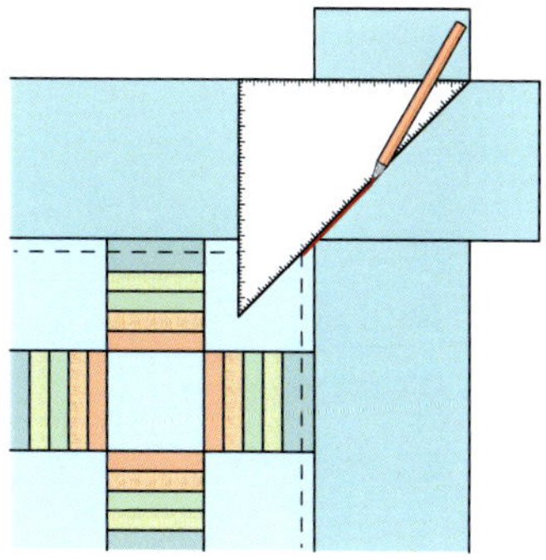

Diagram 2

With right sides together, match the marked seam lines and pin (Diagram 3). Begin at the inside corner and sew the strips together, stitching exactly on the marked lines. Check the right side to see that the corner lies flat. Trim excess fabric, leaving ¼" seam allowance. Press seam open.

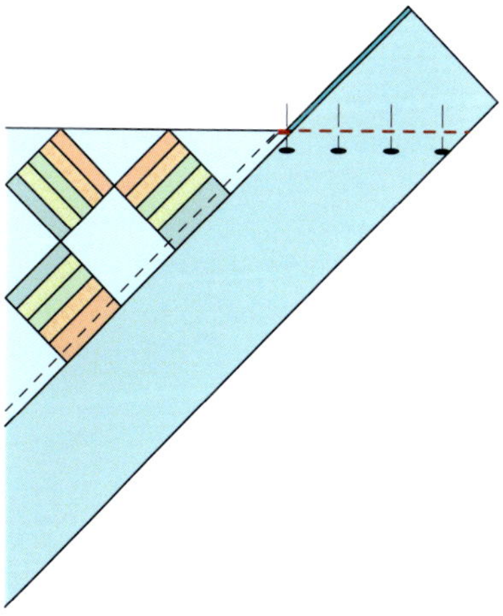

Diagram 3

Quilt It

Now that it's time to put it all together, consider these tips for finishing your quilt.

TIP

To baste layers together, work from the center of the quilt out. Pin or stitch, spacing the pins or stitches 3" to 4" apart.

Choose Your Batting

Batting, *above,* comes in different fibers (cotton, polyester, wool, and silk), and its loft can range greatly—from ⅛" to 1" or more. Generally, choose a low to medium loft for hand or machine quilting and a high loft for tied quilts. Pay attention to the manufacturer's label, which recommends the maximum distance between rows of quilting. If you exceed this distance, the batting will shift and bunch later, resulting in a lumpy quilt.

Assemble the Layers

Cut and piece the backing fabric to measure at least 3" bigger on all sides than the quilt top. Press seams open. Place the quilt backing wrong side up on a large, flat surface. Center and smooth the batting in place atop the quilt backing. Center the quilt top right side up on top of the batting and smooth out any wrinkles. Use safety pins or long hand stitches to baste all the layers together.

Quilt as Desired

Check out a few of the more common machine-quilting methods *opposite.*

TIP

Always refer to the batting package label to see if the batting you're considering is compatible with the amount of stitching you plan to do on your project.

Stitching in the ditch

Stitch just inside a seam line; the stitches should almost disappear into the seam. Using a walking-foot attachment on your sewing machine will help prevent the quilt layers from shifting.

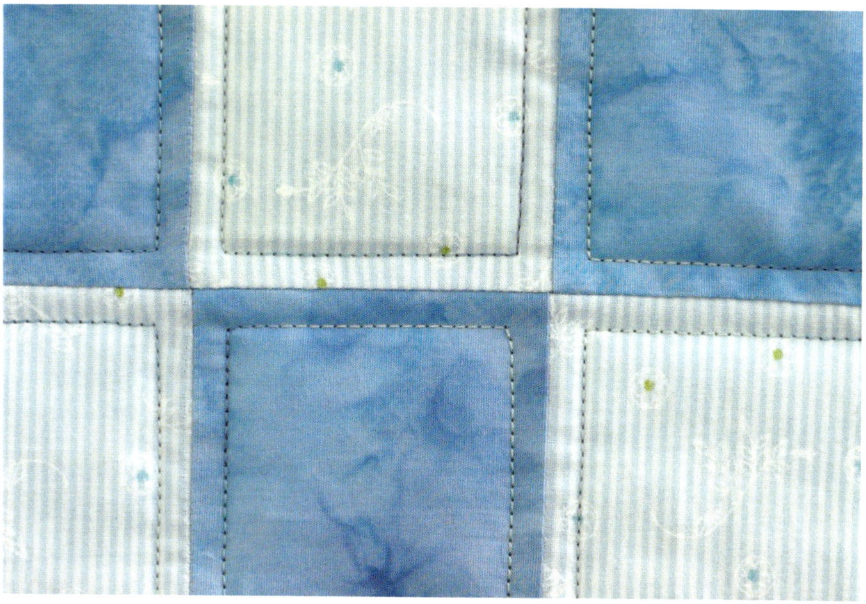

Outline quilting

Stitch ¼" from a seam line or the edge of an appliqué shape, just past the extra thickness of the seam allowance.

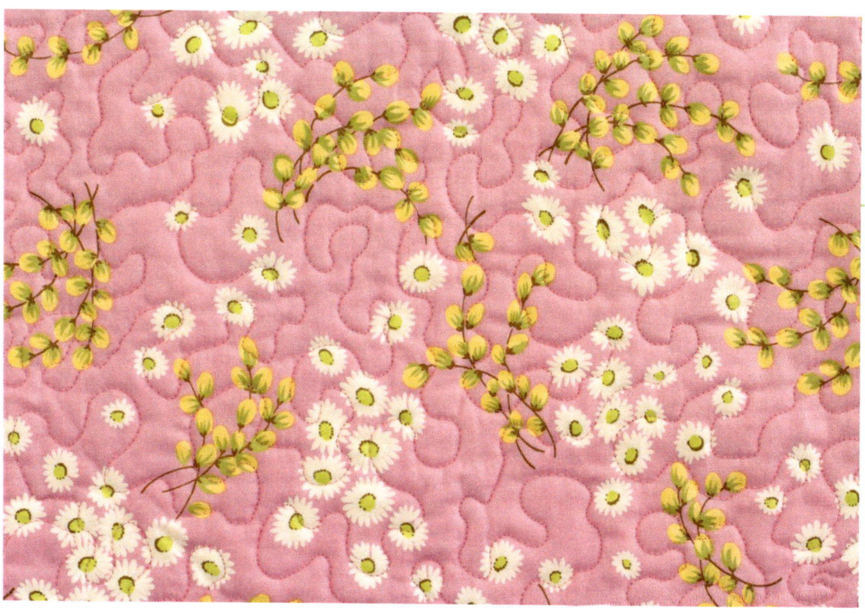

Stipple quilting

This random, allover stitching provides texture and interest behind a pattern. Use a darning foot and lower the feed dogs on your machine.

Top 10 Tips for Machine Quilting

Machine quilting doesn't have to be intimidating. These tips from an expert machine quilter will guide you.

Once you've completed your quilt top, it's time to layer it with batting and backing and then quilt it. For many quilters, the thought of machine quilting can be overwhelming. Take the advice of machine-quilting expert Mabeth Oxenreider, who shares her tips for success. (For more specific quilting how-tos, see Quilt It, *page 16*.)

1. From the start, think about how you want to quilt your project. Knowing how you're going to finish the project can help you make decisions along the way. For example, if you're going to quilt a grid design, you may change the direction you press the seam allowances to avoid quilting over them.

2. Prepare for a smooth quilt back. Use spray starch (according to the manufacturer's directions) on your quilt backing before taping it to the floor or a table. This will give the fabric a firmer hand and make it easier for you to smooth all the layers before pinning. Keep the top, batting, and backing taut (not stretched) as you pin to make quilting easier.

3. Give yourself space. When you sit down to machine quilt, give the quilt as much space as possible. Avoid letting it drop to the floor, as this will create drag on the quilt, causing long, irregular stitches. If you have a limited work surface, adjust an ironing board to the height of your sewing machine bed to help support the quilt's weight.

4. Use the right tools. Select an 80/12 sharp sewing machine needle and 60-weight thread in both the needle and bobbin.

5. Know where you're stitching. If you're stitching in the ditch, the needle should pierce the quilt just next to, but not in, the seam line.

6. Experiment with free-motion quilting. In this type of quilting, you drop the feed dogs and move the fabric freely in all directions beneath a darning foot. Use your hands as a hoop, placing your thumbs about 3" in front of the presser foot and fanning your fingers out to the sides. Never push the fabric ahead; this will cause tucks and wrinkles in your quilting or cause the batting to pull, which distorts the finished quilt. If your machine won't allow you to drop the feed dogs, tape a business card over them to prevent them from grabbing the fabric.

7. Concentrate on the moment. Instead of worrying about the parts of the quilt that are resting on the table, pay attention to the portion of the quilt under your hands.

8. Quilt the straight lines first to keep them straighter. If you've pinned the layers together well, you should be able to start quilting any portion of the quilt.

9. Go slowly when quilting curved designs. Going too fast doesn't give your machine time to make a good stitch. Bobbin thread that is resting on top of the quilt backing is one sign that you may be stitching too fast.

10. Get comfortable and relax. Don't expect every stitch to be like the last one. It isn't possible to make every stitch the same, but with practice you can achieve an overall stitch consistency.

To control bulk while stitching, some quilters use quilt clips to secure the rolled-up edges.

Better Binding

Double-layer binding is easy to apply and adds durability to your finished quilt.

Cut the Strips

The cutting instructions for each project tell you the width and how many binding strips to cut. Unless otherwise specified, cut binding strips on the straight grain of the fabric. Join the binding strips with diagonal seams, *opposite bottom,* to make one long binding strip. Trim seams to ¼" and press open.

Attach the Binding

With the wrong side inside, fold under 1" at one end of the binding strip and press. Then fold the strip in half lengthwise with the wrong side inside. Place the binding strip against the right side of the quilt top along one edge, aligning the binding strip's raw edges with the quilt top's raw edge (do not start at a corner). Begin sewing the binding in place 2" from the folded end.

Photo 1

Photo 2

Photo 3

Turn the Corner

Stop sewing when you're ¼" from the corner (or a distance equal to the seam allowance you're using). Backstitch, then clip the threads (Photo 1). Remove the quilt from under the sewing-machine presser foot.

Fold the binding strip upward, creating a diagonal fold, and finger-press (Photo 2).

Holding the diagonal fold in place with your finger, bring the binding strip down in line with the next edge, making a horizontal fold that aligns with the quilt edge. Start sewing again at the top of the horizontal fold, stitching through all layers (Photo 3). Sew around the quilt, turning each corner like this.

Finish It Up

When you return to the starting point, encase the binding strip's raw edge inside the folded end and finish sewing to the starting point. Trim the batting and backing fabric even with the quilt top edges.

Turn the binding over the edge to the back. Hand-stitch the binding to the backing fabric only, covering any machine stitching. To make the binding corners on the quilt back match the mitered corners on the quilt front, hand-stitch up to a corner and make a fold in the binding. Secure the fold with a couple stitches, then continue stitching the binding in place along the next edge.

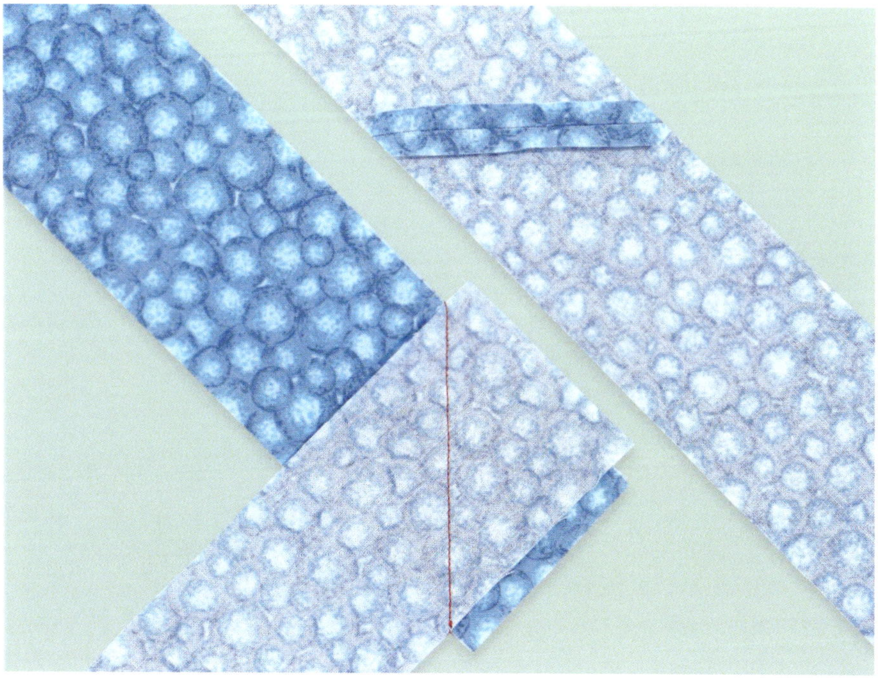

Place binding strips perpendicular to each other and stitch. Trim ¼" beyond seam. After stitching, reduce bulk by pressing the seams open; trim excess.

projects

Easy Four-Patch

Looking for a weekend project? You can make a throw in a jiffy with this Four-Patch block design and a variety of fat-quarter pieces. The larger block size is ideal for showcasing a collection of large-motif prints.

Materials

- 22—18×22" (fat-quarter) assorted prints (blocks)
- ⅔ yard print (binding)
- 4 yards backing fabric
- 77" square batting
- Clear monofilament thread

Finished quilt: 70" square
Finished blocks: 5" square

Quantities are for 44/45"-wide, 100% cotton fabrics. Measurements include a ¼" seam allowance. Sew with right sides together unless otherwise stated.

Designer: Jennifer Keltner
Photographer: Cameron Sadeghpour

Cut Fabrics

From assorted prints, cut:

- 196—5½" squares
- 8—2½×42" binding strips

Assemble Four-Patch Blocks

1. Sew together assorted print 5½" squares in pairs (Four-Patch Block Diagram). Press seams in opposite directions. Join pairs to make a Four-Patch block. Press seam in one direction. The block should be 10½" square, including seam allowances. Repeat to make 49 Four-Patch blocks total.

Four-Patch Block Diagram

Assemble Quilt

1. Lay out all blocks in seven horizontal rows of seven Four-Patch blocks each. Sew together blocks in each row. Press seams in one direction.

2. Join rows to make quilt center. Press seams in one direction. The quilt center should be 70½" square, including seam allowances.

Finish Quilt

1. Layer quilt top, batting, and backing; baste. (For details, see Quilt It, *page 16*.) Quilt as desired.

2. Join assorted print 2½×42" strips to make a pieced binding strip. Bind with pieced binding strip. (For details, see Better Binding, *page 20*.)

TIP

To avoid damage to your sewing machine and injury to yourself, don't sew over pins. Remove each pin right before the machine needle gets to it.

Hourglass Quilt

Created using only fat quarters, this cozy lap quilt is an inviting mix of soft pastel prints and stripes.

Designer: Jennifer Keltner
Photographer: Cameron Sadeghpour

Materials

- 18—18×22" pieces (fat quarters) assorted prints and plaids in coral, pink, cream, and light green (blocks, border, binding)
- 12—18×22" pieces (fat quarters) assorted green and blue prints (quilt backing)
- 58×68" batting

Finished quilt: 51½×62"
Finished block: 10¼" square

Quantities are for 100% cotton fabrics. Measurements include a ¼" seam allowance. Sew with right sides together unless otherwise stated.

When designer Jennifer Keltner made a quilt for her daughter Samantha, she was designing as she went, cutting assorted pieces from a fat-quarter bundle. When the quilt was finished, she had enough setting triangles leftover to create a throw for herself. The resulting quilt uses only fat quarters—even for a contrasting quilt back. (Don't know what a "fat quarter" is? See page 6.)

Cut Fabrics

To make the best use of your fabrics, cut pieces in the following order.

The instructions given are for cutting four triangles from each 11½" square.

From 12 assorted prints and plaids, cut:

- 12—11½" squares, cutting each diagonally twice in an X for 48 triangles total

From 6 assorted prints and plaids, cut:

- 12—10¾" squares

From scraps of assorted prints and plaids, cut:

- 13—2½×21" binding strips
- 46—3¼×5½" rectangles for border

From assorted green and blue prints, cut:

- 12—20×17½" rectangles for backing

Assemble Hourglass Blocks

1. Sew together two nonmatching assorted print or plaid triangles to make a triangle pair (Diagram 1). Press seam in one direction. Repeat with remaining triangles for 24 triangle pairs total; press seam in same direction each time.

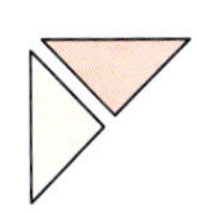

Diagram 1

2. Sew together two triangle pairs to make an hourglass block (Diagram 2). Press seam in one direction. The block should be 10¾" square, including seam allowances. Repeat to make 12 hourglass blocks total.

Diagram 2

Assemble Quilt Top

1. Referring to Quilt Assembly Diagram, lay out hourglass blocks and 12 assorted print and plaid 10¾" squares in six horizontal rows.

2. Sew together blocks in each row. Press seams toward 10¾" squares. Join rows to make quilt center. Press seams in one direction. The pieced quilt center should be 41½×62", including seam allowances.

Assemble and Add Border

1. Referring to Quilt Assembly Diagram, join 23 assorted print and plaid 3¼×5½" rectangles to make a pieced border strip. Trim pieced border strip to 5½×62", including seam allowances. Repeat to make a second pieced border strip.

Quilt Assembly Diagram

2. Sew pieced border strips to long edges of quilt center to complete quilt top. Press seams toward border.

Finish Quilt

1. Referring to Backing Assembly Diagram, lay out assorted green and blue print 20×17½" rectangles in four horizontal rows. Sew together to make pieced backing.

2. Layer quilt top, batting, and pieced backing; baste. (For details, see Quilt It, *page 16*.)

3. Quilt as desired. This quilt is machine-stitched in an allover flower-and-loop pattern.

4. Using diagonal seams, join assorted print and plaid 2½×21" strips to make a pieced binding strip. Bind with pieced binding strip. (For details, see Better Binding, *page 20*.)

Backing Assembly Diagram

Fine Stripes

A perfect baby shower gift, this strip-pieced cutie comes together in a flash using as many prints as you wish.

Designer: Lynette Jensen of Thimbleberries
Photographer: Greg Scheidemann

Materials

- 3 yards total assorted pastel prints (pieced rows)
- 6—$\frac{1}{4}$-yard pieces assorted pastel tone-on-tones (sashing)
- $\frac{1}{2}$ yard light yellow print (binding)
- $2\frac{2}{3}$ yards backing fabric
- 47×60" batting

Finished quilt: $40\frac{1}{2}$×$53\frac{1}{2}$"

Quantities are for 44/45"-wide, 100% cotton fabrics. Measurements include a $\frac{1}{4}$" seam allowance. Sew with right sides together unless otherwise stated.

Strip piecing makes quick work of this adorable crib-size quilt. By first sewing together 42"-long fabric strips, then cutting them into shorter pieces, you minimize the time you have to spend cutting lots of little pieces.

Cut Fabrics

To make the best use of your fabrics, cut pieces in the following order.

From assorted pastel prints, cut:

- 50—42"-long strips in widths varying from 1¼" to 1¾"

From *each* of 2 pastel tone-on-tones, cut:

- 1—2½×41½" sashing strip
- 1—2½×40½" sashing strip

From *each* of 2 more pastel tone-on-tones, cut:

- 1—2½×41½" sashing strip
- 2—2½×4½" sashing rectangles

From *each* of 2 remaining pastel tone-on-tones, cut:

- 1—2½×41½" sashing strip

From light yellow print, cut:

- 5—2½×42" binding strips

Assemble Pieced Units

1. Aligning long edges, sew together five assorted pastel print 42"-long strips to make a strip set (Diagram 1). Press seams in one direction. Repeat to make 10 strip sets total, varying the combinations of prints in each set.

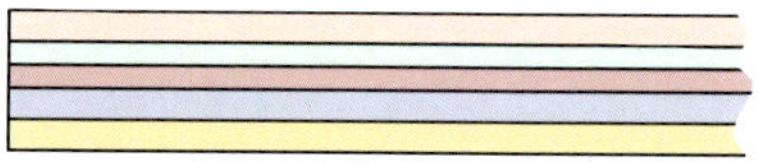

Diagram 1

2. Cut strip sets into ninety 4½"-wide segments total (Diagram 2). The segment lengths will vary depending on the width of the strips used to make the strip sets.

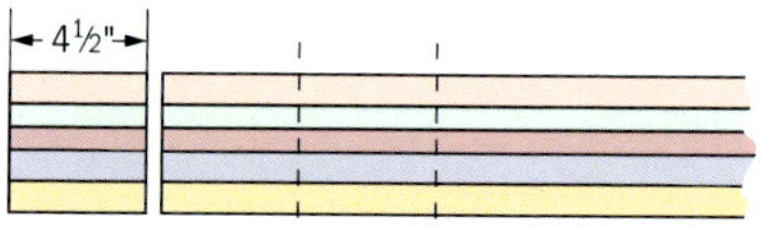

Diagram 2

3. Join and trim assorted-length segments to make the following units. Press seams in one direction. (For a scrappy look, vary the assortment and placement of the segments in each pieced unit.)

- 7—4½×41½" pieced rows
- 2—4½×28½" border units
- 4—4½"-square corner blocks

Assemble Quilt Center

1. Referring to Quilt Assembly Diagram, lay out the seven 4½×41½" pieced rows, alternating them with the six assorted pastel tone-on-tone 2½×41½" sashing strips. The sashing strips with matching 2½×4½" sashing rectangles should be in the far left-hand and far right-hand positions.

2. Join strips to make quilt center. Press seams toward sashing strips. The quilt center should be 40½×41½", including seam allowances.

Add Borders

1. Join assorted pastel tone-on-tone 2½×40½" sashing strips to top and bottom edges of quilt center. Press seams toward sashing strips.

2. Referring to Quilt Assembly Diagram, join two 4½"-square corner blocks, two pastel tone-on-tone 2½×4½" sashing rectangles, and a 4½×28½" border unit in a row to make a border strip. (Pay attention to color placement of pastel sashing rectangles that will appear to extend from sashing strips in quilt center.) Press seams toward sashing rectangles. The border strip should be 4½×40½", including seam allowances. Repeat to make a second border strip.

3. Join border strips to top and bottom edges of quilt center, matching pastel tone-on-tone sashing rectangles to quilt center sashing strips, to complete the quilt top. Press seams toward sashing strips.

Finish Quilt

1. Layer quilt top, batting, and backing; baste. (For details, see Quilt It, *page 16*.)

2. Quilt as desired. This project was machine-quilted with an allover meandering design atop the pieced strips and blocks. A wavy line was stitched over each sashing strip and sashing rectangle seam line.

3. Bind with light yellow binding strips. (For details, see Better Binding, *page 20*.)

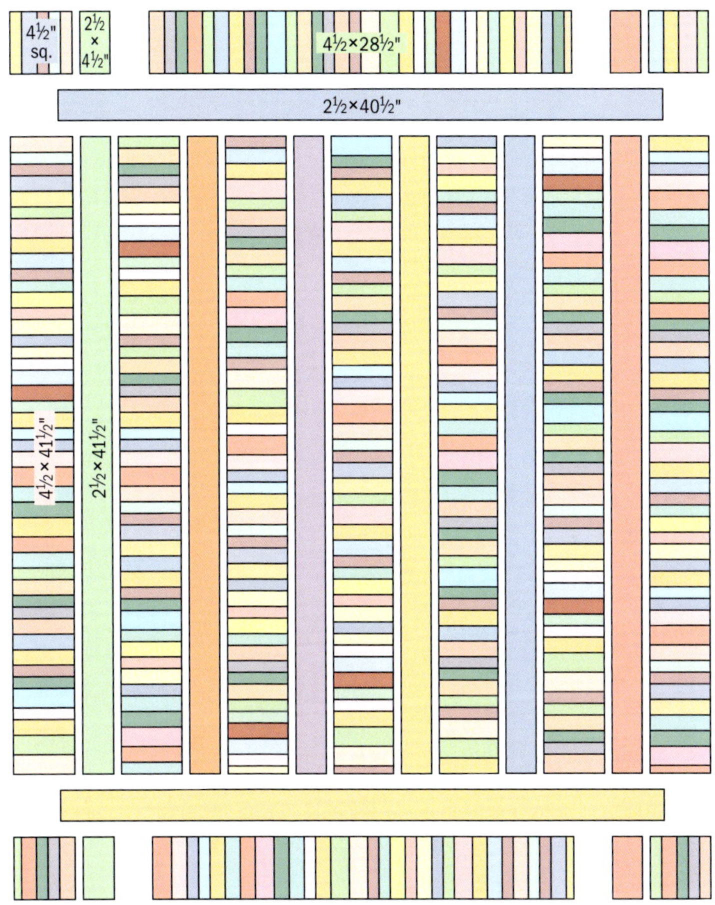

Quilt Assembly Diagram

TIP

For a less scrappy version, use three colors, such as orange, blue, and yellow. Alternate colors in the strip-pieced rows and use a single color for sashing strips.

Pillow Trio

Make a sophisticated style statement on a budget with these classy accent pillows.

Materials

Patchwork Pillow:

- ¼ yard red dot (block)
- ¼ yard gold print (block)
- ¼ yard green print (block)
- 1 yard multicolor floral (block, pillow back)
- ¼ yard green stripe (binding)
- 21" square muslin
- 21" square batting
- 18"-square pillow form

Stripe Pillow:

- ¼ yard green stripe (block)
- ⅛ yard dark red print (block)
- ⅔ yard red dot (block, pillow back)
- 19" square muslin
- 19" square batting
- 16" square pillow form

Appliqué Pillow:

- ¼ yard gold dot (block)
- ⅔ yard multicolor floral (block, pillow back)
- ¼ yard green print (border, appliqués)
- ¼ yard dark red print (appliqués)
- 19" square muslin
- 19" square batting
- 16" square pillow form
- Lightweight fusible web

Finished pillows:
patchwork pillow, 18" square;
stripe pillow and appliqué pillow, 16" square

Quantities are for 44/45"-wide fabrics. Unless otherwise specified, measurements include a ¼" seam allowance. Sew with right sides together unless otherwise stated.

Designer: Lynette Jensen of Thimbleberries
Photographer: Greg Scheidemann

Taking a modern approach to living room decor, Lynette Jensen came up with these three accent pillows. One uses simple patchwork, another strip piecing, and the third combines patchwork and appliqué. All show off her hallmark—deceptively simple design.

Cut and Assemble Patchwork Pillow

To make the best use of your fabrics, cut the pieces in the following order.

From red dot, cut:
- 2—6¾×8¾" rectangles

From gold print, cut:
- 2—4¾×6½" rectangles
- 2—2½×6¾" rectangles

From green print, cut:
- 2—6¾×8¾" rectangles

From multicolor floral, cut:
- 2—19×23" rectangles
- 1—6½×10½" rectangle

From green stripe, cut:
- 2—3×42" binding strips

1. Referring to Patchwork Pillow Assembly Diagram, lay out rectangles in three rows. Sew together pieces in each row. Press seams in one direction, alternating direction with each row. Join rows to make pillow top. Press seams in one direction.

2. Layer pillow top with batting and muslin square; baste. Quilt as desired. (For details, see Quilt It, *page 16*.) Trim batting and backing even with pillow top edges.

3. With wrong side inside, fold each multicolor 19×23" rectangle in half to form two double-thick 19×11½" rectangles. (The double thickness makes the pillow back more stable.) Overlap folded edges of double-thick rectangles by about 4" to make a 19" square (Pillow Back Assembly Diagram). Baste ½" from edges to make pillow back.

4. Layer pillow top and back wrong sides together; join with ½" seam. Bind with green stripe binding strips using ½" seams. (For details, see Better Binding, *page 20*.) Insert pillow form through opening.

Patchwork Pillow Assembly Diagram

Pillow Back Assembly Diagram

projects

Cut and Assemble Stripe Pillow

To make the best use of your fabrics, cut the pieces in the following order.

From green stripe, cut:
- 2—4½×16½" rectangles

From dark red print, cut:
- 2—1½×16½" rectangles

From red dot, cut:
- 2—16½×20½" rectangles
- 1—6½×16½" rectangle

1. Referring to Stripe Pillow Assembly Diagram, lay out rectangles. Sew together pieces to make pillow top. Press seams in one direction.

2. Layer pillow top with batting and muslin square; baste. Quilt as desired. (For details, see Quilt It, *page 16*.) Trim batting and backing even with pillow top edges.

Stripe Pillow Assembly Diagram

3. Using red dot 16½×20½" rectangles and referring to Cut and Assemble Patchwork Pillow, Step 3, on page 31, assemble pillow back.

4. Layer pillow top and back. With right sides together, join with a ¼" seam. Turn right side out. Insert pillow form through opening.

Cut and Assemble Appliqué Pillow

To make the best use of your fabrics, cut the pieces in the following order. Patterns are shown *opposite*. To use fusible web for appliquéing, complete the following steps. (For more information on fusible appliqué, see Fabric Appliqué, opposite.)

1. Lay fusible web, paper side up, over patterns. Use a pencil to trace each pattern the number of times indicated in cutting instructions, leaving at least ½" between tracings. Cut out each fusible-web shape roughly ¼" outside traced lines.

2. Following manufacturer's instructions, press fusible-web shapes onto backs of designated fabrics; let cool. Cut out fabric shapes on drawn lines and peel off paper backings.

From gold dot, cut:
- 3—4½×8½" rectangles

From multicolor floral, cut:
- 2—16½×20½" rectangles
- 3—4½" squares

From green print, cut:
- 2—2½×16½" border strips
- 2—2½×12½" border strips
- 3 of Pattern B

From dark red print, cut:
- 3 of Pattern A

1. Referring to Appliqué Pillow Assembly Diagram, lay out gold dot rectangles and multicolor floral squares in three rows. Sew together pieces in each row. Press seams toward multicolor floral squares. Join rows to make block. Press seams in one direction.

2. Aligning long edges, join green print short border strips to opposite edges of block. Add green print long border strips to remaining edges to make pillow top. Press all seams toward border.

3. Referring to Appliqué Pillow Assembly Diagram, position three dark red print A flowers and three green print B flower centers onto the pillow top. Fuse the pieces in place and machine-blanket-stitch with black thread.

4. Layer pillow top with batting and muslin square; baste. Quilt as desired. (For details, see Quilt It, *page 16*.) Trim batting and backing even with pillow top edges.

5. Using multicolor floral 16½×20½" rectangles and referring to Cut and Assemble Stripe Pillow, steps 3 and 4, left, assemble pillow back and finish appliqué pillow.

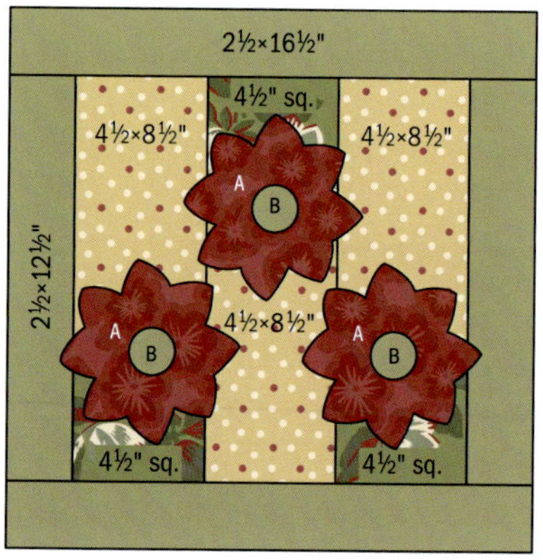

Appliqué Pillow Assembly Diagram

FABRIC APPLIQUÉ

Try Fusible Appliqué

Instead of using a needle and thread, secure cutout appliqué shapes with an iron-on adhesive—often called fusible web. Many fast-and-easy appliqué projects are meant to be fused, then secured with stitching. Follow the directions in the project instructions for how to prepare appliqué pieces for fusing.

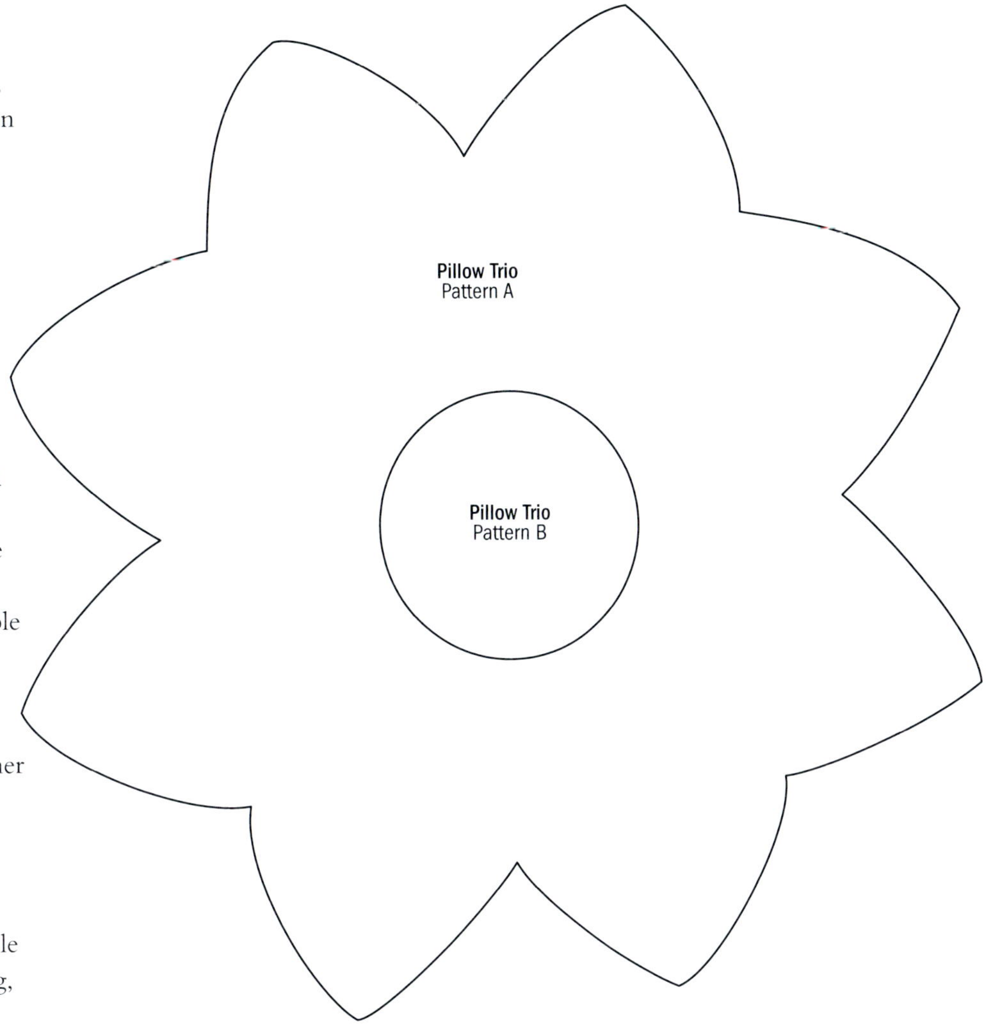

Choose a Fusible Web

Choose a lightweight, paper-backed fusible web that can be stitched through unless you plan to leave the appliqué edges unfinished. In that case, use heavyweight, no-sew fusible web. It's important to follow the manufacturer's instructions for adhering the fusible web because factors like iron temperature, whether or not to use steam, and length of pressing time can vary by brand.

Finish the Edges

A common finishing stitch for fusible appliqué is a narrow machine zigzag, *bottom left*. Position the machine presser foot so the left swing of the needle will land on the appliqué shape and the right swing of the needle will land on the foundation, just on the outer edge of the appliqué shape. To produce uniform machine-appliqué stitches, sew at a slow, even pace. Another common option is a blanket stitch, either by machine, *bottom center*, or by hand, *bottom right*.

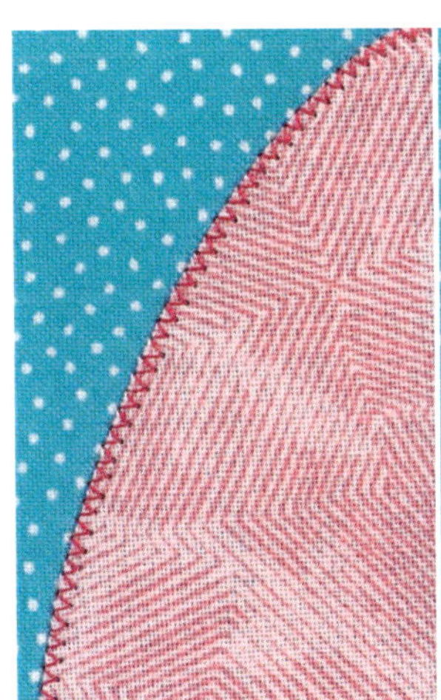
Zigzag Stitch

Machine Blanket Stitch

Hand Blanket Stitch

Plaid Nine-Patch

Plaid flannel creates visual interest and appealing texture in this simple-to-sew quilt.

Materials

- $1\frac{1}{2}$ yards orange-and-green plaid flannel (blocks, setting squares, border)
- $\frac{3}{8}$ yard blue star print flannel (blocks)
- 22" square tan plaid (binding)
- $1\frac{1}{4}$ yards backing fabric
- 42" square quilt batting

Finished quilt: $35\frac{3}{4}$" square
Finished block: $8\frac{1}{4}$" square

Quantities are for 44/45"-wide, 100% cotton fabrics. Measurements include a $\frac{1}{4}$" seam allowance. Sew with right sides together unless otherwise stated.

Designer: Terry Clothier Thompson
Photographer: Hopkins Associates

Through thoughtful cutting methods, designer Terry Clothier Thompson maximized the impact of an orange-and-green plaid. The quilt's border features strips cut on the straight grain, while the setting squares sport a bias cut. For the Nine-Patch blocks, Terry fussy-cut the orange-and-green plaid so that each block contains two predominantly orange and two predominantly green squares. (Fussy-cutting means cutting out a specific print or motif from a piece of fabric.)

Cut Fabrics

To make the best use of your fabrics, cut the pieces in the order that follows. You may wish to cut your strips longer than specified to allow for possible sewing differences. Cut the 20 plaid 3¼" squares so that 10 are mostly orange plaid and 10 are mostly green plaid.

From orange-and-green plaid flannel, cut:

- 4—6×30¾" border strips
- 4—8¾" squares cut on the bias (For details, see Cutting on the Bias, *page 12.*)
- 20—3¼" squares

From blue star print flannel, cut:

- 25—3¼" squares

From tan plaid, cut:

- Enough 2½"-wide bias strips to total 160" in length for binding (For details, see Cutting on the Bias.)

Assemble Nine-Patch Blocks

1. Referring to Block Assembly Diagram, lay out five blue star print 3¼" squares, two mostly orange plaid 3¼" squares, and two mostly green plaid 3¼" squares in three vertical rows. Sew together squares in each row. Press seams toward blue star print squares.

Block Assembly Diagram

projects

2. Join rows to make Nine-Patch block. Press seams toward center row. Nine-Patch block should be 8¾" square, including seam allowances.

3. Repeat steps 1 and 2 to make five Nine-Patch blocks total.

Assemble Quilt Top

1. Referring to Quilt Assembly Diagram, lay out five Nine-Patch blocks and four orange-and-green plaid 8¾" setting squares in three rows. For added interest, rotate two Nine-Patch blocks 90°.

2. Sew together pieces in each row. Press seams in one direction, alternating direction with each row. (When sewing and pressing the setting squares, be careful not to stretch the bias edges.)

3. Join rows to make quilt center. Press seams in one direction. Pieced quilt center should be 25¼" square, including seam allowances.

4. Referring to Quilt Assembly Diagram, place an orange-and-green plaid 6×30¾" border strip on top edge of quilt center, with strip's left edge extending 5½" left of quilt center. Sew together, leaving 7" unsewn at top left corner. Sew a second orange-and-green plaid 6×30¾" border strip to right-hand edge of quilt center. Working clockwise around quilt, sew border strips to remaining edges. Finish sewing top border seam to complete quilt top. Press all seams toward border.

Quilt Assembly Diagram

Finish Quilt

1. Layer quilt top, batting, and backing; baste. (For details, see Quilt It, *page 16*.)

2. Quilt as desired. A 1¼"-wide diagonal grid stitched across the quilt top complements the angles in the Nine-Patch blocks and plaid squares.

3. Bind with tan plaid bias strips. (For details, see Better Binding, *page 20*.)

Star Wall Hanging

Learn the trick to making star blocks the easy way when you piece this simple big-block throw.

Materials

- ½ yard white print
- 3—18×22" pieces (fat quarters) three assorted green prints (blocks, border)
- 3—18×22" pieces (fat quarters) three assorted blue prints (blocks, border)
- 6—18×22" pieces (fat quarters) assorted pink prints (blocks, border)
- ⅓ yard blue floral (binding)
- 1¼ yards backing fabric
- 43" square batting

Finished quilt: 36" square
Finished block: 12" square

Quantities are for 44/45"-wide, 100% cotton fabrics. Measurements include a ¼" seam allowance. Sew with right sides together unless otherwise stated.

Designer: Allison Jane Smith of Plaids and Prints
Photographer: Craig Anderson

Cut Fabrics

To make the best use of your fabrics, cut pieces in the following order.

From white print, cut:

- 48—3½" squares

From *each* assorted green and blue print, cut:

- 16—3½" squares

From assorted pink prints, cut:

- 32—3½" squares

From blue floral, cut:

- 4—2½×42" binding strips

Assemble Blocks

There are various methods for making triangle-squares, a basic unit used in many quilts. To simplify the cutting process, this construction method allows you to make all of the blocks using only 3½" squares.

1. For one star block, you'll need 12 white print 3½" squares and eight pairs of matching print 3½" squares (two pairs *each* from assorted blue and green prints and four pairs from assorted pink prints).

2. With wrong side inside, fold a white print 3½" square in half diagonally; press. Unfold and place atop a pink print 3½" square. Sew together on pressed line. Trim excess, leaving ¼" seam allowance (Diagram 1). Press open to make a white triangle-square (Diagram 2).

Diagram 1

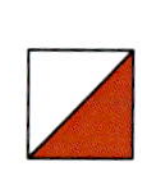
Diagram 2

3. Using two 3½" squares *each* from green and blue prints and three additional pink print 3½" squares, repeat Step 2 to make eight white triangle-squares total.

4. Using remaining green, blue, and pink print 3½" squares, repeat Step 2 to make two pink-and-green triangle-squares and two blue-and-pink triangle-squares total.

5. Referring to Block Assembly Diagram, lay out all triangle-squares and the remaining four white print 3½" squares in four rows.

Block Assembly Diagram

6. Sew together pieces in each row. Press seams in one direction, alternating direction with each row. Join rows to make an Eight-Pointed Star block. Press seams in one direction. The block should be 12½" square, including seam allowances.

7. Repeat steps 1 through 6 to make four Eight-Pointed Star blocks total.

Assemble Quilt Center

1. Lay out Eight-Pointed Star blocks in two horizontal rows (Quilt Assembly Diagram).

2. Sew together blocks in each row. Press seams in one direction, alternating direction with each row. Join rows to complete quilt center. Press seams in one direction. The quilt center should be 24½" square, including seam allowances.

Assemble and Add Border

1. Referring to Quilt Assembly Diagram, join six assorted pink, green, and blue print 6½" squares to make a long border strip. Press seams in one direction. Repeat to make a second long border strip.

2. Sew together four assorted pink, green, and blue print 6½" squares to make a short border strip. Press seams in one direction. Repeat to make a second short border strip.

3. Sew short border strips to opposite sides of quilt center. Add long border strips to remaining edges to complete quilt top. Press all seams toward border.

Quilt Assembly Diagram

Finish Quilt

1. Layer quilt top, batting, and backing; baste. (For details, see Quilt It, *page 16*.) Quilt as desired.

2. Bind with blue floral strips. (For details, see Better Binding, *page 20*.)

TIP

Nobody's perfect! To ease in a bit of extra fullness when the lengths of two pieced units don't quite match, sew with the longer unit on the bottom.

Bow-Tie Quilt

Making Bow-Tie blocks is much easier than you may think, especially with this fool-the-eye trick for easy piecing.

Materials

- 6—18×22" pieces (fat quarters) assorted dark polka dots (blocks)
- 6—18×22" pieces (fat quarters) assorted light polka dots (blocks, middle border)
- $1\frac{1}{2}$ yards solid white (sashing, inner border)
- $1\frac{2}{3}$ yards purple print (sashing, outer border, binding)
- $4\frac{7}{8}$ yards backing fabric
- 64×86" batting

Finished quilt: $57\frac{1}{2}$×80"
Finished block: 6" square

Quantities are for 44/45"-wide, 100% cotton fabrics. Measurements include a ¼" seam allowance. Sew with right sides together unless otherwise stated.

Designer: Karen Snyder
Photographer: Greg Scheidemann

Fat-quarter bundles are always hard for designer Karen Snyder to pass up. For this quilt, she used a bundle of six coordinating pairs of polka dots. Her quick method of making Bow-Tie blocks works best with small-scale and nondirectional prints.

Cut Fabrics

To make the best use of your fabrics, cut pieces in the following order. These cutting instructions allow for very little fabric waste with the light polka dots; buy additional fat quarters if desired.

From *each* dark polka dot, cut:
- 18—3½" squares
- 18—1½" squares

From one light polka dot, cut:
- 3—2¼×22" strips for middle border
- 18—3½" squares

From *each* remaining light polka dot, cut:
- 2—2¼×22" strips for middle border
- 18—3½" squares

From solid white, cut:
- 6—2×42" strips for inner border
- 93—2×6½" sashing rectangles

From purple print, cut:
- 7—4×42" strips for outer border
- 8—2½×42" binding strips
- 40—2" sashing squares

Assemble Blocks

1. Use a pencil to draw a diagonal line on wrong sides of dark polka dot 1½" squares. (To prevent fabric from stretching as you draw the lines, place 220-grit sandpaper under the squares.)

2. Align a marked dark polka dot 1½" square with one corner of a coordinating light polka dot 3½" square (Diagram 1; note direction of drawn line). Sew on marked line. Trim excess, leaving ¼" seam allowance; press open attached triangle to make a pieced unit. Repeat to make 108 pieced units total.

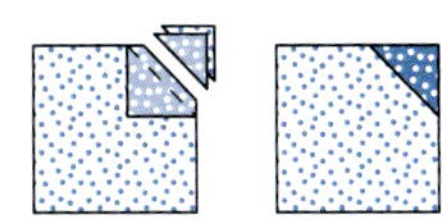

Diagram 1

3. Referring to Diagram 2, sew together two matching pieced units and two matching dark polka dot 3½" squares in pairs. Press seams in opposite directions. Join pairs to make a Bow-Tie block. Press seam in one direction. The block should be 6½" square, including seam allowances. Repeat to make 54 Bow-Tie blocks total.

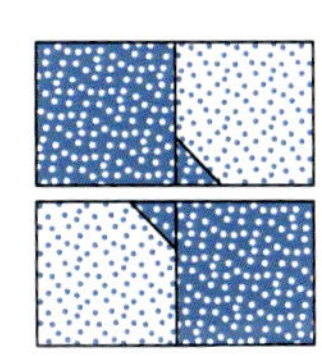

Diagram 2

Assemble Quilt Center

1. Referring to Quilt Assembly Diagram, lay out Bow-Tie blocks, 93 solid white sashing rectangles, and 40 purple print sashing squares in 17 horizontal rows.

2. Sew together pieces in each row. Press seams toward Bow-Tie blocks and sashing squares. Join rows to make quilt center. Press seams in one direction. The quilt center should be 44×66½", including seam allowances.

Assemble and Add Borders

Cut and piece solid white 2×42" strips to make:

- 2—2×66½" inner border strips
- 2—2×47" inner border strips

1. Sew long inner border strips to quilt center's long edges. Add short inner border strips to remaining edges. Press all seams toward border.

2. Beginning and ending with the same color of light polka dot, join the 13 assorted light polka dot 2¼×22" strips with diagonal seams to make one long pieced strip.

Cut long pieced strip in the following order to make:

- 1—2¼×69½" middle border strip No. 1
- 1—2¼×48¾" middle border strip No. 2
- 1—2¼×71¼" middle border strip No. 3
- 1—2¼×50½" middle border strip No. 4

1. Beginning with left-hand edge, sew middle border strips to quilt center in numerical order (Quilt Assembly Diagram). Press all seams toward middle border.

Cut and piece purple print 4×42" strips to make:

- 2—4×73" outer border strips
- 2—4×57½" outer border strips

1. Sew long outer border strips to quilt center's long edges. Sew short outer border strips to remaining edges to complete quilt top. Press all seams toward outer border.

Quilt Assembly Diagram

Finish Quilt

1. Layer quilt top, batting, and backing; baste. (For details, see Quilt It, *page 16*.)

2. Quilt as desired. This project features an allover stipple pattern across the quilt top.

3. Bind with purple print binding strips. (For details, see Better Binding, *page 20*.)

Lazy Dayz Tote

Stitch up an appealing bag that's the perfect size for carefree weekend days.

Materials

- 18×22" piece (fat quarter) pink print (triangle-squares, band, bag base)
- 18×22" piece (fat quarter) dark pink print (triangle-squares, lining)
- ¼ yard light green print (Four-Patch units)
- ¼ yard green print (Four-Patch units, bag handle)
- ⅛ yard green polka dot (Four-Patch units)
- ⅓ yard muslin (backing)
- 16×26" thin batting
- 3×9" piece of heavy cardboard

Finished bag: 9×9×3"

Quantities are for 44/45"-wide, 100% cotton fabrics. Measurements include a ¼" seam allowance. Sew with right sides together unless otherwise stated.

Designer: Cindy Taylor Oates
Photographer: Greg Scheidemann

When choosing fabrics for the miniature patchwork pieces that make up this bag, select mostly small-scale prints. For more style, consider using a specialty fabric, such as silk douppioni, for the solid band or the entire bag.

If you want a more secure bag, think about adding a closure, such as ribbon ties, a button and loop, or magnetic snaps.

Cut Fabrics

To make the best use of your fabrics, cut pieces in the following order.

From pink print, cut:
- 1—3½×9½" rectangle
- 2—2×12½" rectangles
- 20—2⅞" squares

From dark pink print, cut:
- 2—9½×12½" rectangles
- 1—3½×9½" rectangle
- 20—2⅞" squares

From light green print, cut:
- 4—1¼×42" strips

From green print, cut:
- 2—1¼×42" strips
- 2—2×18½" strips for handles

From green polka dot, cut:
- 2—1¼×42" strips

From muslin, cut:
- 2—9½×12½" rectangles
- 1—3½×9½" rectangle

From thin quilt batting, cut:
- 2—9½×12½" rectangles
- 1—3½×9½" rectangle

Assemble Triangle-Squares

1. Use a quilter's pencil to mark a diagonal line on wrong side of each pink print 2⅞" square. (To prevent fabric from stretching as you draw lines, place 220-grit sandpaper under the squares.)

2. Layer a marked pink print 2⅞" square atop each dark pink print 2⅞" square. Sew each pair together with two seams, stitching ¼" on each side of drawn line (Diagram 1).

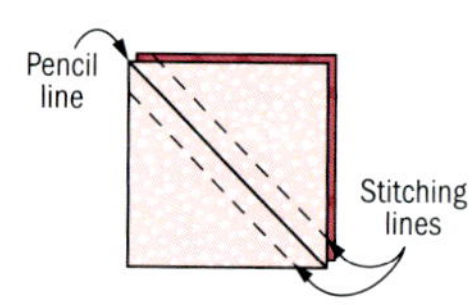

Diagram 1

3. Cut each pair apart on drawn line to make two triangle units (Diagram 2). Press each triangle unit open, pressing seam toward dark pink triangle, to make 40 triangle-squares total (Diagram 3). Each triangle-square should be 2" square, including seam allowances.

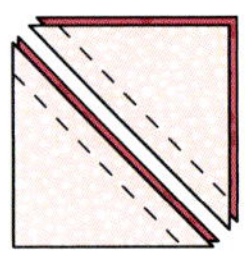
Diagram 2

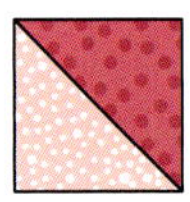
Diagram 3

Assemble Four-Patch Units

1. Join a light green print 1¼×42" strip and a green print 1¼×42" strip to make a strip set (Diagram 4). Press seam toward darker print. Repeat to make a second strip set; cut strip sets into forty 1¼"-wide segments total.

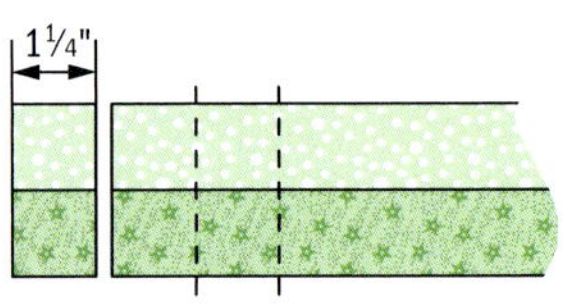

Diagram 4

2. Sew together two 1¼"-wide segments to make a Four-Patch unit A (Diagram 5). Press seam in one direction. The unit should be 2" square, including seam allowances. Repeat to make 20 Four-Patch A units total.

Diagram 5

3. Repeat steps 1 and 2 using two green polka dot 1¼×42" strips and remaining light green print 1¼×42" strips to make 20 Four-Patch B units total.

Assemble Bag Front and Back

1. Referring to Diagram 6, lay out a pink print 2×12½" rectangle, 20 triangle-squares, 10 Four-Patch A units, and 10 Four-Patch B units in six horizontal rows. Pay attention to how Four-Patch units A and B are placed to create diagonal rows of the same units.

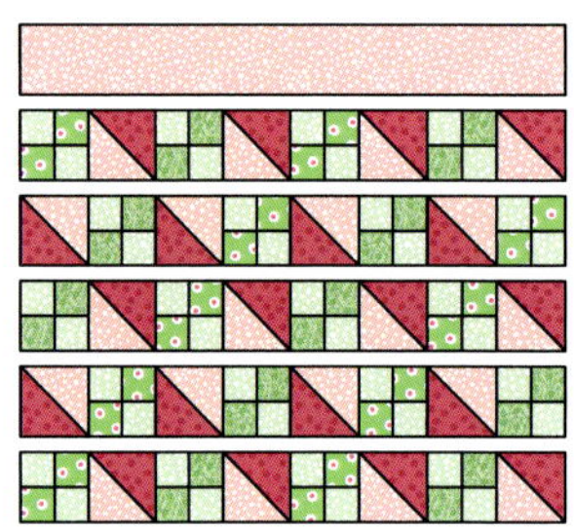
Diagram 6

2. Sew together pieces in each row. Press seams toward triangle-squares. Join rows to make bag front; press seams in one direction.

3. Repeat steps 1 and 2 to make the bag back.

Assemble Outer Bag

1. Layer bag front with batting and muslin 9½×12½" rectangles. Baste layers a scant ¼" from all edges. Quilt as desired. (This bag is machine-quilted with an allover stipple.) Repeat with bag back.

2. Layer pink print 3½×9½" rectangle with batting and muslin 3½×9½" rectangles. Baste layers a scant ¼" from all edges to make the bag base. Quilt as desired.

3. Mark center bottom of bag front and back. Mark center of each long edge of the bag base (Diagram 7).

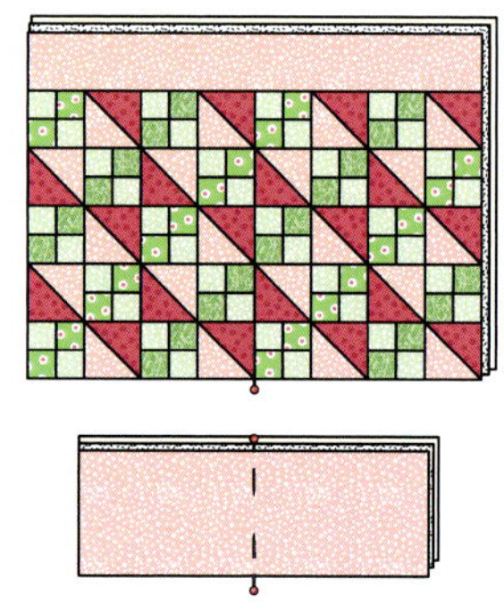
Diagram 7

4. Matching centers, sew bag base to bag front and back (Diagram 8). Press seams toward bag base. Topstitch bag base through all layers, about ⅛" from seams.

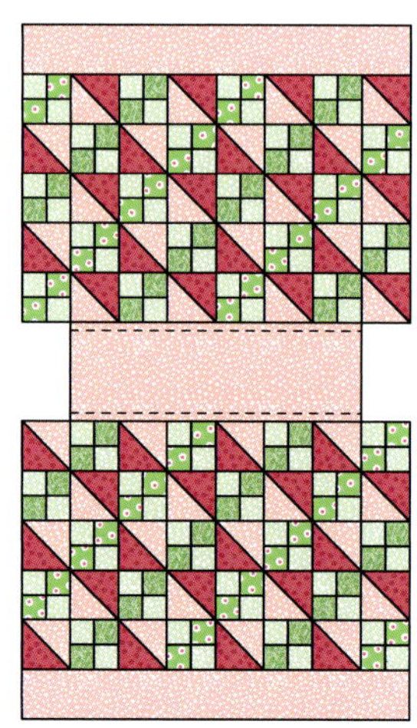
Diagram 8

5. Fold both green print 2×18½" strips in half lengthwise with right sides inside; stitch along long edges. Trim seams to ⅛" and turn right sides out. Press flat and topstitch ⅛" from long edges to make two handles.

6. Pin handles to top of bag front and back with ends about 2¼" from side edges; baste (Diagram 9).

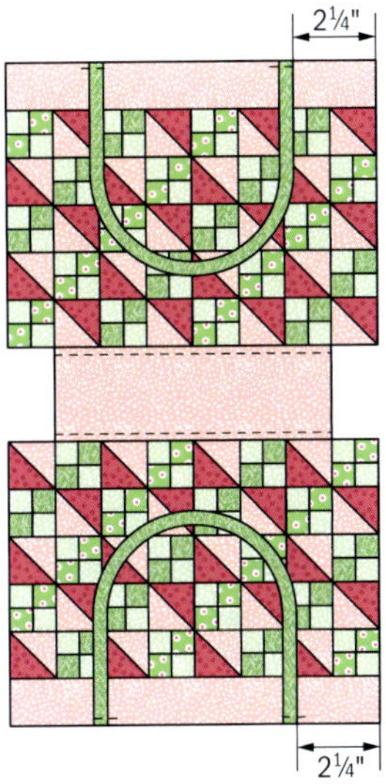

Diagram 9

7. Sew bag front to bag back along sides; press seams open. Mark center of each short edge of the bag base with a pin. Fold bag so one pin matches the corresponding side seam (Diagram 10). Stitch across end of bag. Repeat with other side of bag to complete outer bag.

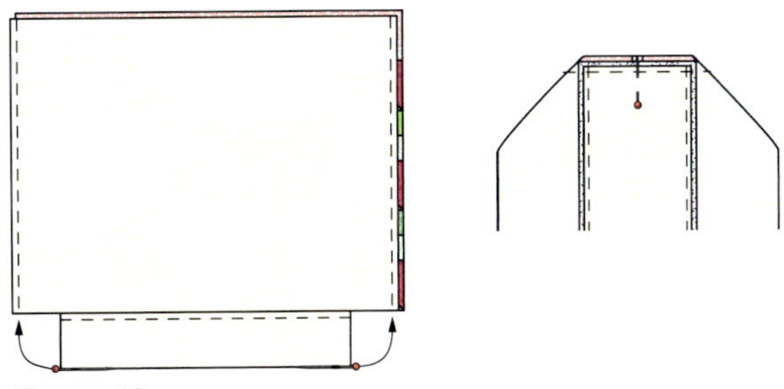
Diagram 10

Assemble Lining

1. Mark center bottom of dark pink print 9½×12½" rectangles. Mark center of each long edge of dark pink print 3½×9½" rectangle. Matching centers, sew large rectangles to small rectangle to make lining; press seams toward small rectangle. Topstitch small rectangle through all layers about ⅛" from seams.

2. Sew together sides of bag lining, leaving a 5" opening for turning on one side. Press seams open. Mark center of each short edge of lining base with a pin. Referring to Diagram 10, fold lining so one pin matches corresponding side seam. Stitch across end of lining. Repeat with other side of lining.

Finish Bag

1. Place lining inside outer bag with right sides together and side seams matching. Stitch along top edges. Turn bag right side out through opening in lining. Slip-stitch opening closed. Smooth lining inside bag. Press bag's upper edge and topstitch ⅛" from edge.

2. For a sturdier bag, place a 3×9" piece of heavy cardboard in bottom of bag.

TIP

Experiment with your bag design just by rearranging the pieces and turning them in different ways.

Better Homes and Gardens® Creative Collection™

Editorial Director John Riha

Editor in Chief Deborah Gore Ohrn

Executive Editor Karman Wittry Hotchkiss

Managing Editor Kathleen Armentrout

Contributing Editorial Manager Heidi Palkovic

Contributing Design Director Tracy DeVenney

Contributing Editor Laura Holtorf Collins
Contributing Designer Wendy Musgrave
Copy Chief Mary Heaton
Contributing Copy Editor Mary Helen Schiltz
Proofreader Joleen Ross
Administrative Assistant Lori Eggers

Publishing Group President
Jack Griffin
Executive Vice President
Doug Olson

Meredith CORPORATION

President and CEO Stephen M. Lacy

Chairman of the Board William T. Kerr

In Memoriam
E. T. Meredith III (1933–2003)
